Washing

Travel Guide

2023-2024

Exploring the Iconic Landmarks of the Nation's Capital

Bruce Terry

Bruce Terry

Bruce Terry

MAP OF WASHINGTON DC

Bruce Terry

Bruce Terry

Bruce Terry

Bruce Terry

INTRODUCTION

Welcome to Washington, D.C., the dynamic capital of the United States! A treasure wealth of history, culture, and political significance can be found in the center of this busy metropolis. Prepare to be enthralled by renowned buildings, world-class museums, and a unique blend of tradition and innovation as you travel across the nation's capital in 2023-2024.

With famous monuments such as the stately U.S. Capitol, the historic White House, and the solemn Lincoln Memorial, Washington, D.C. serves as a living testament to the rich fabric of American democracy. As you walk around the National Mall, you will be surrounded by the majesty of the Washington Monument and tributes to great leaders who molded the future of the nation.

But Washington, D.C. is more than just a political and power center. It is a cultural paradise with a remarkable collection of world-class museums and art galleries. The Smithsonian Institution alone houses multiple museums devoted to subjects ranging from natural history and space exploration to American art and African American history. Immerse yourself in the wealth of information and artistic expression that these hallowed halls have to offer.

Washington, D.C., beyond the official corridors of power and the hallowed halls of museums, is a lively city brimming with vitality. Diverse restaurants, fashionable boutiques, and a busy nightlife animate the districts. Explore Georgetown's cobblestone lanes, which lead to attractive stores and old architecture. Delight your taste buds in Dupont Circle's thriving restaurant scene or explore the city's numerous cultural districts.

Whether you're a history buff, an art connoisseur, a foodie, or simply an avid traveler looking for new experiences, Washington, D.C. will leave an everlasting imprint on your journey. Prepare to go on an incredible journey through America's heart and soul. This Washington, D.C. travel guide for 2023-2024 will be your dependable companion, highlighting the hidden jewels and must-see sights that will make your trip unforgettable. Allow the charm of the nation's capital to unfurl before your eyes as you immerse yourself in its history, traditions, and the spirit of a unified nation.

HISTORY

Washington, D.C. was formed on July 16, 1790, as a result of President George Washington's signature on the Residence Act. The legislation sought to establish a permanent capital for the nascent nation as a symbol of unity as well as a practical answer to the thorny problem of capital location. The site chosen by Pierre Charles L'Enfant along the Potomac River between Maryland and Virginia was approved, and the city was named after the first president.

L'Enfant's Design: Pierre Charles L'Enfant, a French architect, and engineer, devised the city's famous layout. His idea included vast boulevards, great squares, and radial avenues, resulting in a one-of-a-kind urban plan that highlighted the city's grandeur. L'Enfant's design included the Capitol Building (placed at the east end of the National Mall) and the President's House (now known as the White House).

Early Development during the War of 1812: Washington, D.C. grew rapidly in the early nineteenth century. The erection of significant government buildings, such as the United States Treasury and the United States Patent and Trademark Office, cemented the city's status as the nation's administrative center. During the War of 1812, however, the British stormed the city and destroyed several important structures, including the White House and the Capitol. This incident exposed the capital's vulnerability, prompting upgrades in its security and infrastructure.

Slavery and Emancipation: Washington, D.C., like much of the rest of the country at the time, had a complicated relationship with slavery. Slavery was lawful in the district until President Abraham Lincoln signed the Compensated Emancipation Act on April 16, 1862, which abolished slavery in the area and compensated slaveholders. Thousands of fugitive slaves seeking freedom and security sought refuge in the city during the Civil War.

Reconstruction and Post-Civil War Washington, D.C.: Following the Civil War, Washington, D.C. entered a period of reconstruction and transformation. With the erection of key government buildings such as the Library of Congress, the Supreme Court, and the Washington Monument, the city witnessed rapid growth. During this period, African Americans had an important part in defining the city's cultural and political scene, with famous figures like Frederick Douglass and Booker T. Washington influencing the fight for civil rights.

Civil Rights Movement and Political Evolution: Washington, D.C. became a focal place for the civil rights movement during the twentieth century. Martin Luther King Jr. delivered his famous "I Have a Dream" address from the steps of the Lincoln Memorial during the historic March on Washington in 1963. The incident aided in the passage of legislation such as the Civil Rights Act of 1964 and the Voting Rights Act of 1965, both of which attempted to abolish racial discrimination.

Modern Washington, D.C.: As a global city, Washington, D.C. has evolved in recent decades. It has seen a tremendous revival, with programs involving economic development, cultural expansion, and urban redevelopment altering diverse districts. The city's diversified population, flourishing arts scene, and burgeoning gastronomic landscape all contribute to its distinct personality.

Bruce Terry

WEATHER AND CLIMATE

Geographical Factors: Washington, D.C. is located in the humid subtropical climate zone, which has hot and humid summers, mild winters, and heavy precipitation all year. The city is located at a latitude of around 38.9 degrees north and an elevation of approximately 410 feet (125 meters) above sea level. These geographical considerations contribute to the region's distinct climate.

Seasonal Summary:

Spring (March to May): The transition from winter to summer in Washington, D.C. is generally warm. During this season, temperatures steadily rise, with typical highs ranging from the mid-50s°F (about 12°C) in March to the mid-70s°F (24-26°C) in May. Spring, on the other hand, can be unpredictable, with temperature swings and varied precipitation amounts.

Summer (June to August): Summers in Washington, D.C. are warm and muggy, reaching their peaks in July and August. Temperatures in the upper 80s°F (30-32°C) are common, with highs occasionally exceeding 90°F (32°C). High humidity levels can make the weather feel even more miserable. Thunderstorms are prevalent in the summer, giving relief from the heat but occasionally resulting in severe rain.

Bruce Terry

Autumn (September to November): The season in Washington, D.C. is distinguished by cooler weather and vibrant foliage. Summer heat persists in September, with average highs in the mid-70s°F (24-26°C). Temperatures generally decline as the season passes, with highs in the mid-50s°F (12-14°C) by November. Autumn is often seen as a pleasant season, with decreasing humidity and sporadic rain showers.

Winter (December to February): Winters in Washington, D.C. are milder than in some northern cities, although they can still bring cold spells and snowfall. In December and January, average high temperatures range from the mid-40s°F (7-9°C) to the low 50s°F (10-12°C) in February. Temperatures can, however, fluctuate, and cold bursts can send temperatures below freezing. Snowfall is unpredictable, however, it usually falls multiple times during the winter months.

Precipitation: Washington, D.C. experiences moderate rainfall all year, with an annual average of around 40 inches (1,000 mm). Rainfall is distributed fairly evenly, while it is significantly heavier in the summer months due to increased thunderstorm activity. Snowfall is less common, however, it can occur from December through February. Every year, the city receives about 15 inches (38 cm) of snow.

Bruce Terry

Extreme Weather: Washington, D.C. is vulnerable to a variety of extreme weather phenomena. During the summer, the city may be hit by severe thunderstorms, which are occasionally accompanied by strong winds, heavy rain, and hail. Tornadoes are uncommon, but not unheard of. In the winter, the city is occasionally hit by nor'easters, which bring heavy snowfall and high winds. However, in comparison to locations further north, these phenomena are rather rare.

10 REASONS WHY YOU SHOULD VISIT WASHINGTON DC

Historical Importance: Washington, D.C. is rich in history, making it a must-see trip for history buffs. Every area of the city has a tale to tell, from the National Mall, where you'll discover iconic landmarks like the Lincoln Memorial and the Washington Monument, to the neighboring Arlington National Cemetery, where the nation's heroes are laid to rest.

Iconic Landmarks: The city is home to some of the world's most iconic landmarks. The stately United States Capitol, White House, and Supreme Court are emblems of American democracy that can be explored on guided tours. Furthermore, the Jefferson Memorial, the Martin Luther King Jr. Memorial, and the Vietnam Veterans Memorial are just a few of the city's moving tributes to historical individuals and events.

Bruce Terry

Smithsonian Institution: The world-renowned Smithsonian Institution, the world's largest museum and research complex, is located in Washington, D.C. There is an abundance of knowledge and cultural experiences waiting to be discovered with 19 museums and galleries, including the National Air and Space Museum, the National Museum of Natural History and American history.

Washington, D.C., being the seat of political power in the United States, provides a unique perspective on the country's governance. You may learn about the legislative process, explore the Library of Congress, and even sit in on a congressional session by visiting the U.S. Capitol Visitor Center. Furthermore, the interactive Newseum offers an intriguing viewpoint on the role of media in democracy.

A Diverse and Lively Cultural Landscape: Washington, D.C. has a diverse and lively cultural landscape. The John F. Kennedy Center for the Performing Arts, which produces world-class theater, ballet, and music performances, is located in the city. The National Theatre, Ford's Theatre, and Warner Theatre provide a variety of artistic experiences as well. Furthermore, the city's areas, such as Georgetown and Adams Morgan, are bursting at the seams with art galleries, stylish shops, and delectable dining options.

Outdoor Spaces: There are several options to enjoy the outdoors in Washington, D.C. The National Mall is a large green space ideal for picnics, jogging, or simply strolling while admiring the spectacular views. Rock Creek Park has miles of hiking and bike routes, and the Tidal Basin is a beautiful setting, especially during cherry blossom season in the spring.

World-Class Educational Organizations: Several famous universities and research organizations, including Georgetown University and George Washington University, are located in the city. These institutions contribute to the intellectual and cultural vibrancy of the city by holding public events, seminars, and exhibitions.

Diversity and Worldwide Influence: Washington, D.C. is a cultural melting pot with worldwide influences. The city's streets are lined with embassies and diplomatic posts from all over the world, adding to its international feel. Chinatown and Dupont Circle, for example, are dynamic areas that provide various cuisines, cultural festivals, and one-of-a-kind shopping experiences.

Festivals & Events: Washington, D.C. offers several festivals and events all year round, drawing visitors from all over the world. The National Cherry Blossom Festival, the Smithsonian Folklife Festival, and the Fourth of July celebrations on the National Mall are just a few of the thrilling events that display the city's energy and variety.

Easy Access to Nearby Attractions: Because it is located on the East Coast, Washington, D.C. provides easy access to other fascinating

Bruce Terry

sites. You can visit the historic metropolis of Philadelphia or the picturesque town of Annapolis, Maryland on a day trip. Furthermore, the city's central location makes it convenient to travel to other big cities such as New York and Boston.

Bruce Terry

CHAPTER 1

GENERAL INFORMATION

• POPULATION

Washington currently has a population of 7.17 million people, and significant growth is predicted to continue. Although Washington is the 13th most populous state in the US, it is only the 25th most densely populated. There are 101.2 persons for every square mile of Washington State territory in its total area of 71,299 square miles.

Seattle is the state's largest city, with a population of 684,451 and a population density of 7,962 persons per square mile. Contrarily, the Seattle-Tacoma-Bellevue metropolitan area, which has 3.73 million residents, also includes the neighboring towns of Kent, Tacoma, Bellevue, and Everett. It is home to more than half of the people in the state. King and Pierce counties in Washington State have the highest populations, with 2,188,649 and 876,764 people, respectively.

• PUBLIC HOLIDAY

New Year's Day: New Year's Day, observed on January 1st, celebrates the beginning of the New Year in Washington, D.C. Many travelers throng to the city to experience the historic New Year's Eve festivities and the yearly fireworks show at the National Mall. On New Year's Day, various attractions, such as museums and government buildings, may be closed or operate on limited hours. However, the city's iconic landmarks like the Washington Monument and Lincoln Memorial remain available for outdoor exploring.

Martin Luther King Jr. Day: Martin Luther King Jr. Day is marked on the third Monday in January, remembering the life and achievements of the civil rights leader. This national holiday provides an opportunity to engage in memorial events and visit major historical locations associated with the civil rights movement. The Martin Luther King Jr. Memorial, located near the National Mall, is a must-visit attraction, offering a powerful tribute to Dr. King's legacy.

Presidents' Day: Presidents' Day is commemorated on the third Monday in February, recognizing the efforts of past U.S. presidents. During this holiday, many government offices, schools, and companies are closed, resulting in crowded attractions. You can explore historic sites like the White House, the U.S. Capitol, and the National Archives, but expect lengthier lines and additional security measures owing to the flood of visitors.

Memorial Day: Memorial Day, commemorated on the final Monday in May, is a day of remembrance for the men and women who died while serving in the U.S. armed services. In Washington, D.C., Memorial Day is honored by different events, including parades, concerts, and wreath-laying ceremonies. The National Memorial Day Parade, situated along Constitution Avenue, is a notable feature. Additionally, you can pay your respects at the serious and affecting memorials, such as the Vietnam Veterans Memorial and the Arlington National Cemetery.

Independence Day: Independence Day, celebrated on July 4th, is one of the most exuberant public holidays in Washington, D.C. The city comes alive with patriotic fervor and stages the famed "A Capitol Fourth" concert on the West Lawn of the U.S. Capitol, followed by a stunning fireworks show over the National Mall. It's vital to plan, as the area gets highly congested. Many museums and attractions may have reduced schedules or close early on this day.

Labor Day: Labor Day, marked on the first Monday in September, honors the American labor movement and the contributions of workers to the country's success. The long weekend is a wonderful time to explore the city's many districts, enjoy outdoor activities in the parks, and visit prominent museums like the Smithsonian Institution, the National Gallery of Art, and the International Spy Museum. However, be aware that certain businesses and restaurants may have shortened hours or limited services on this occasion.

Thanksgiving: Thanksgiving, observed on the fourth Thursday in November, is a time for family to gather together and express appreciation. In Washington, D.C., the Thanksgiving Day Parade, held along Constitution Avenue, is a cherished tradition, featuring floats, marching bands, and gigantic balloons. Many restaurants in the city provide special Thanksgiving menus, allowing tourists to taste a traditional holiday dinner. It's advisable to make appointments in advance, as popular establishments might fill up rapidly.

Christmas Day: Christmas Day, commemorated on December 25th, is a day for celebration and reflection. Washington, D.C., adorns itself with festive decorations, including the National Christmas Tree near the White House. Many sites, such as the Smithsonian museums, may be closed or operate on limited hours on Christmas Day. However, you may still enjoy the lovely ambiance by wandering through the city's brightly illuminated streets and visiting outdoor ice skating rinks, such as the National Gallery of Art Sculpture Garden Ice Rink.

• ELECTRIC PLUG

Voltage in Washington, D.C.: The standard voltage in Washington, D.C. is 120 volts. This voltage corresponds to the electrical system used in the United States. If you are traveling from a place where the voltage is different, ensure sure your electronic equipment is suitable. Most current electronic gadgets, such as laptops and smartphones, have voltage converters built in that can handle a wide range of voltages. Certain products, such as hair dryers and electric shavers, may require a voltage converter or transformer.

Type A and Type B electric plugs are used in Washington, D.C., and the rest of the United States. Type A plugs have two parallel flat pins, whereas Type B plugs have an additional grounding pin in the form of a round or U-shaped prong. It's crucial to remember that the majority of sockets in the United States support both Type A and Type B plugs, so you should be fine without an adaptor.

Adapters and converters: If your country uses a different type of plug, you'll need a plug adapter to connect your gadgets to the outlets in Washington, D.C. Plug adapters can be obtained at most travel stores or online before your trip. These adapters merely allow you to connect your device to local power outlets. But remember that plug adapters don't change voltage. If your devices are not 120-volt compatible, you will also require a voltage converter or transformer to protect your equipment.

International Visitors: International visitors to Washington, D.C. should be aware that the United States operates on a 60 Hz electrical frequency. Some products, such as clocks, electric motors, and some medical devices, may not function properly if your country employs a different frequency (e.g., 50 Hz). A frequency converter may be required in such instances. Most modern electrical gadgets, such as

Bruce Terry

laptops and smartphone chargers, are intended to work with both 50 Hz and 60 Hz frequencies, so you should have no problems.

Additional Suggestions:

It's usually a good idea to bring a universal plug converter that can fit different plug types, guaranteeing you can charge your electronics no matter where you go.

Many hotels in Washington, D.C. provide power outlets with USB connections, allowing you to charge your gadgets without the need for a plug adapter.

Consider packing a power strip if you intend to use many electronic gadgets at the same time. This allows you to charge several gadgets from a single outlet.

• CURRENCY

The official currency of the United States is the dollar (USD). The dollar is represented by the sign "$" and is further subdivided into cents, with coins in denominations of one cent (penny), five cents (nickel), ten cents (dime), and twenty-five cents (quarter), as well as paper bills in denominations of one, five, ten, twenty, fifty, and one hundred dollars. When visiting Washington, D.C., bring a combination of cash and credit cards to accommodate various payment scenarios.

Bruce Terry

Currency Exchange: If you need to exchange your currency for US dollars, Washington, D.C. has a variety of possibilities. Banks, currency exchange offices, and hotels are all typical sites to exchange currencies. Banks typically offer competitive exchange rates, however, their hours of operation may be limited. Currency exchange offices, on the other hand, may keep extended hours and are more likely to be found in busy tourist destinations. To guarantee you get the greatest value, compare rates and fees before making any trade.

Banking Facilities: Washington, D.C. is home to various national and international banks, making banking facilities easily accessible during your visit. Most banks have ATMs where you can withdraw cash using your debit or credit card. ATMs are available across the city, particularly at airports, shopping malls, and popular tourist destinations. You must notify your bank of your trip plans to avoid problems with your cards while overseas.

Credit and Debit Cards: Because credit and debit cards are widely accepted in Washington, D.C., they are easy payment methods. Visa, Mastercard, American Express, and Discover credit cards are generally accepted in hotels, restaurants, stores, and tourist sites. Most locations that accept credit cards accept debit cards with the Visa or Mastercard logo. However, carrying cash is always a good idea for smaller sellers or venues that may not accept cards.

Bruce Terry

Traveler's checks: While they were once widespread, they have become less common in recent years. Many stores and restaurants in Washington, D.C. no longer accept traveler's checks, so it's best to use credit cards or cash instead.

Tipping Etiquette: Tipping is traditional in the United States, and Washington, D.C. is no exception. Tipping service providers such as waitstaff, taxi drivers, tour guides, and hotel staff are customary. The standard rule of thumb for tipping is 15% to 20% of the total bill, while certain places may automatically include a service charge. Before tipping, always check the bill to determine if a service charge has been applied.

• LANGUAGE

Official Language: English is the official language of Washington, D.C., and the United States. Throughout the city, English is commonly spoken and understood. English is the major language used in government agencies, corporations, and educational settings. The local populace speaks English well, making it simple for visitors to interact and explore the city.

Spanish: Due to the considerable Hispanic and Latino population of Washington, D.C., Spanish is the second most commonly spoken language. The city has a thriving Latino community, with many residents coming from El Salvador, Mexico, and Guatemala. Spanish is spoken in a variety of neighborhoods, restaurants, stores, and cultural events. Bilingual signage and services are frequently available, catering to the needs of guests who speak Spanish.

Other Commonly Spoken Languages:

Washington, D.C. is a cultural melting pot that attracts individuals from all over the world. As a result, many languages are spoken across the city. Other widely spoken languages include:

a) *Chinese:* With a significant Chinese community, notably in the Chinatown neighborhood, many residents speak Mandarin and Cantonese. Visitors can sample real Chinese cuisine and attend cultural programs honoring Chinese traditions.

b) *French:* There are French-speaking populations in Washington, D.C. from France, Canada, and several African nations. Visitors may encounter French speakers in diplomatic circles, cultural groups, and establishments influenced by France.

c*) Amharic:* Because of the city's large Ethiopian population, many residents speak Amharic. The city is well-known for its Ethiopian restaurants and cultural activities, which allow visitors to learn about this East African country's rich history.

d) *Arabic:* There is a sizable Arab community in Washington, D.C., representing numerous Arabic-speaking countries. Arabic is spoken in areas such as Adams Morgan and Georgetown, as well as in diplomatic and government circles.

Bruce Terry

e) *Korean:* As the Korean population grows, Korean-speaking communities can be found in areas such as Annandale, Virginia, just outside of Washington, D.C. Visitors can sample authentic Korean cuisine and participate in Korean cultural events.

Language Services and Resources:

Because of the city's linguistic diversity, various language services and resources are offered to visitors. These are some examples:

a) *Translation and Interpretation Services:* The city's many translation and interpretation organizations provide language help for a variety of purposes, including document translation, on-site interpretation, and telephone interpretation.

b) *Multilingual Tour Guides:* Some tour firms employ multilingual tour guides who may deliver tours in languages such as Spanish, Chinese, and French, among others.

c) *Language Schools and Cultural Centers:* Visitors who want to study a language or learn about different cultures can locate language schools and cultural centers that offer lessons, workshops, and activities to help them improve their linguistic and cultural knowledge.

d) *Bilingual Maps and signs:* Certain areas of the city, particularly those frequented by tourists, may have bilingual maps and signs in

Bruce Terry

different languages, allowing visitors to navigate and find their way about more easily.

• VISA REQUIREMENT

Visa Exemption Program: Before digging into visa criteria, it's vital to determine whether you qualify for the Visa Exemption Program. The Visa Waiver Program (VWP) permits people of selected nations to travel to the United States for vacation or commercial purposes without acquiring a visa, providing they meet particular conditions. As of 2023, 39 countries participate in the VWP, including the United Kingdom, France, Germany, Japan, South Korea, and Australia. Travelers from VWP countries can stay in the U.S. without a visa for up to 90 days. However, it's vital to secure an approved Electronic System for Travel Authorization (ESTA) before your trip.

Non-Immigrant Visas: If you don't qualify for the Visa Exemption Program, you will need to apply for a non-immigrant visa. The type of visa necessary for your travel to Washington, D.C., depends depend on the purpose of your trip. the following list of popular non-immigrant visa categories:

B-1 Visa (Business Visitor): The B-1 visa is suited for those traveling to Washington, D.C., for business-related objectives, such as attending conferences, meetings, or negotiating contracts. To

Bruce Terry

qualify, you must establish that your visit is transitory and that you have adequate means to cover your expenses.

B-2 Visa (Tourist Visitor): If your aim for the trip is tourism, leisure, or visiting friends and family in Washington, D.C., the B-2 visa is appropriate. You should offer evidence of your plan to return to your native country, such as proof of job or property ownership.

F-1 Visa (Student): Students wanting to study at an educational institution in Washington, D.C., should apply for an F-1 visa. You will need to get an acceptance letter from a recognized educational school and verify that you have sufficient means to cover your tuition costs and living expenses.

J-1 Visa (Exchange Visitor): The J-1 visa is designed for those participating in approved exchange programs, including research scholars, instructors, and students. The sponsoring organization must issue a Form DS-2019, which you will need for your visa application.

H-1B Visa (Temporary Worker): If you have a work offer from a U.S. business in Washington, D.C., in a specialist subject requiring theoretical or technical expertise, you may be qualified for an H-1B visa. The employer must file a petition on your behalf, and the quantity of H-1B visas is subject to an annual cap.

Bruce Terry

Visa Application Process:

To apply for a non-immigrant visa for Washington, D.C., follow these steps:

Complete the Online Application: Visit the U.S. Department of State's website and complete the Nonimmigrant Visa Electronic Application (DS-160) form accurately, supplying all the essential information.

Pay the Application Fee: Pay the non-refundable visa application fee, which varies depending on the visa type and place of origin. Keep the receipt, as you will need it for the immigration interview.

Make an Appointment for a Visa Interview: Make a reservation for a visa interview at the closest U.S. embassy or consulate. Prepare the appropriate documents, including your passport, DS-160 confirmation sheet, application fee receipt, and any supporting documents specific to your visa category.

Attend the Interview: On the designated date, attend the visa interview and present your documents. The consular officer will analyze your eligibility and ask questions regarding your purpose of travel, ties to your home country, and financial capabilities.

Wait for Visa Issuance: After the interview, the consular officer will choose whether to approve or deny your visa application. If granted, your passport will be returned to you with the visa affixed inside.

Bruce Terry

Important Tips:

Begin the visa application procedure well in advance of your scheduled travel dates to provide extra time for processing and potential delays.

Ensure all your supporting documents are accurate, up-to-date, and relevant to your visa category.

Provide precise and succinct responses during the visa interview, establishing your ties to your home country and your intention to return.

Maintain patience and cooperation throughout the entire visa application procedure.

• DIETARY RESTRICTIONS AND EATING

Understanding Food Restriction:

Intolerances and allergies:

Washington, D.C. has a diverse food scene that can accommodate a wide range of allergies and intolerances. Many restaurants have extensive expertise dealing with common sensitivities such as gluten, dairy, nuts, and shellfish.

Prioritize explaining your dietary requirements to servers and chefs so that they understand your restrictions and can take the appropriate precautions.

Bruce Terry

Vegan and vegetarian diets:

Washington, D.C. has a plethora of vegetarian and vegan-friendly restaurants, making it simple to obtain plant-based meals. Vegetarian and vegan alternatives are frequently featured on the menus of many eateries.

Fancy Radish, Shouk, and Equinox are among the city's most popular vegan and vegetarian eateries.

Diets that are Kosher or Halal:

Various eateries in Washington, D.C. cater to persons who follow kosher or halal diets.

Char Bar, Sunflower Vegetarian Restaurant, and Eli's Restaurant are kosher-friendly restaurants. Consider The Halal Guys and Naf Naf Grill for halal alternatives.

Gluten-Free Eating Plans:

Gluten-free dining is becoming more widely available in Washington, D.C., with many restaurants offering gluten-free menu items or making modifications on request.

Among the notable eateries that provide gluten-free offerings are Founding Farmers, District Taco, and Rise Bakery.

Bruce Terry

Other Particular Diets:

People who follow certain diets such as paleo, low-carb, or ketogenic can find suitable food options in Washington, D.C.

True Food Kitchen, Protein Bar & Kitchen, and Khepra's Raw Food Juice Bar are restaurants that cater to these dietary needs.

How to Eat in Washington, D.C.:

Plan ahead of time by conducting research.

Before your vacation, look up restaurants and their menus online to identify places that meet your dietary needs.

To read reviews and gather information, use websites and apps such as Yelp, TripAdvisor, and Happy Cow (for vegetarian and vegan options).

Communicate Your Dietary Requirements:

Inform the staff about your dietary restrictions when making a reservation or visiting a restaurant. They can offer advice, recommend appropriate dishes, and make arrangements.

Seek Local Information and Recommendations:

Consult locals or online forums for restaurant recommendations that cater to special dietary needs.

Bruce Terry

Locals are frequently knowledgeable about hidden gems and lesser-known restaurants with special menus.

Farmer's markets and specialty shops:

There are various farmer's markets and specialty stores in Washington, D.C. where you can purchase fresh produce, gluten-free products, organic ingredients, and other items that meet your dietary needs.

For a variety of possibilities, consider visiting Eastern Market, Dupont Circle Farmers Market, or Whole Foods Market.

• CYBER CAFES

The Rise of Cyber Cafés: In an age when connection and digital interactions rule our lives, cyber cafés have arisen as a popular location for people looking for a productive and convivial setting outside of traditional office facilities. As a powerhouse for innovation and technology, Washington, DC has a broad assortment of cyber cafés that cater to the requirements of locals, visitors, and digital nomads alike.

Services and amenities:

a. *High-Speed Internet:* Reliable and high-speed internet access is an essential aspect of every cyber café. To satisfy their work or pleasure needs, visitors may expect seamless browsing, streaming, and video conferencing capabilities.

b. *Workstations and Meeting Rooms*: Most cyber cafés have comfortable workstations with ergonomic chairs, plenty of desk space, and charging ports. Some cafés also include private meeting rooms with audiovisual equipment, which are great for joint projects or business meetings.

c. *Printing and Scanning Services*: Many cyber cafés in Washington, DC provide on-site printing, scanning, and photocopying services, making it easy for professionals who need tangible copies of documents or presentations.

d. *Refreshments:* To boost productivity, cyber cafés frequently provide a variety of beverages, including freshly prepared coffee and specialty teas, as well as energy drinks and snacks. Some establishments also collaborate with local bakeries or cafés to provide a broader assortment of refreshments.

Popular Washington, DC Cyber Cafés:

a. *Wired Bean:* Wired Bean, located in the center of downtown, is a quaint cyber café recognized for its warm ambiance and gourmet coffee. It attracts both freelancers and casual visitors due to its rustic décor and free Wi-Fi.

Bruce Terry

b. *Byte Hub:* Byte Hub is a trendy cyber café near Dupont Circle that caters to tech-savvy workers. It has high-speed internet, cutting-edge workstations, and a contemporary interior design that encourages innovation.

c. *Digital Haven:* As one of the city's largest cyber cafés, Digital Haven provides a huge and well-equipped workspace. Its handy location near a metro station, as well as its range of services, such as printing and private meeting rooms, make it a popular choice among digital nomads.

d. *Connect Café:* Connect Café, located in the trendy Adams Morgan district, combines the attractiveness of a conventional coffee shop with the utility of a cyber café. Its welcoming atmosphere, dependable internet, and shared tables make it a perfect location for networking and cooperation.

Etiquette & principles:

It is critical to follow certain principles when visiting cyber cafés in Washington, DC to preserve a pleasant environment for all patrons. Some general guidelines are as follows:

a. *Respect Quiet Zones:* Many cyber cafés have designated quiet zones for visitors looking for a quiet working environment. In these places, it is critical to avoid loud conversations or disruptive activity.

Bruce Terry

b. *Purchase Requirements:* Some cyber cafés may have a minimum purchase requirement to access their services. This policy ensures that customers contribute to the establishment while using its services.

c. *Tidiness and Cleanliness:* Visitors should maintain cleanliness and tidiness by properly disposing of waste and keeping workstations clean for the next user.

d. *Respect Other Customers' Privacy*: Cyber cafés frequently draw a broad collection of people. It is critical to respect others' privacy by not peering at or commenting on their screens or activities.

• LOCAL TIME

The Eastern Time Zone (ET) is where Washington, D.C. is located. During standard time, the Eastern Time Zone is UTC-5:00, and during daylight saving time, it is UTC-4:00. The time zone is shared by numerous major US East Coast cities, including New York, Boston, and Atlanta.

Daylight Saving Time: Daylight Saving Time (DST) is observed in Washington, D.C. DST begins on the second Sunday of March, when clocks are advanced by one hour, and concludes on the first Sunday of November when clocks are reverted by one hour. The local time is changed from Eastern Standard Time (EST) to Eastern

Bruce Terry

Daylight Time (EDT) during DST, resulting in longer daylight hours in the evenings.

Getting the Local Time:

Several credible sources can be used to ascertain the current local time in Washington, D.C.:

Use online time converters, which allow you to enter your present location and get the matching local time in Washington, D.C. These converters take into account time zone and DST adjustments to ensure accuracy.

Smartphone Apps: Many smartphone apps provide real-time local time updates based on your present location or city of choice. World Clock, Time Zone Converter, and Clocks are popular applications.

World Clocks: Use your smartwatch, computer, or wall clock to check the time in multiple time zones. Adjust the displayed time to reflect the local time in Washington, D.C.

Tips for Managing Time While in Washington, D.C.: Understanding the local time in Washington, D.C. is critical for efficiently arranging your activities and getting the most out of your vacation. Here are some time management suggestions:

Flight and Transportation: When booking flights or making transportation arrangements, keep the local time in mind to ensure you arrive on time. If you are going from another region, keep in mind any time zone variances.

Schedules for Events and Activities: Check the local time to ensure you arrive on time for scheduled events, tours, or activities. Washington, D.C. has many cultural, historical, and political attractions, and being on time will enhance your visit.

Museum and Monument Hours: Check the opening and closing times of the museums and monuments you intend to visit, as they may change throughout the year. During peak tourist seasons, some attractions may offer longer hours, allowing you to make the most of your stay.

Public transit: Learn about the local transit timetables, including bus, rail, and metro operating hours. These timetables are subject to change on weekends, holidays, and special events, so prepare accordingly.

CHAPTER 2

BEST TIME TO VISIT WASHINGTON DC

Spring (March to May): Spring is a popular season for visiting Washington, D.C. The cherry blossoms, which bloom in late March or early April, are a key magnet for people from all over the world. The Tidal Basin and the National Mall are surrounded by cherry blossom trees that are in full bloom. However, because of its popularity, the city can become congested, and hotel prices tend to climb. If you intend to travel during the cherry blossom season, reserve your accommodations well in advance. Spring weather is generally nice, with temperatures ranging from 50°F (10°C) to 70°F (21°C).

Summer (June to August): Summer in Washington, D.C. may be hot and humid, with temperatures regularly reaching the upper 80s°F (about 30°C) or more. During this time of year, the city is crowded with tourists, particularly families on summer vacation. The benefit of traveling during the summer is that you can enjoy extended daylight hours and participate in outdoor activities and events.

The Smithsonian museums and other indoor attractions also offer welcome relief from the heat. It's worth noting that some residents leave the city around August, making it significantly less crowded. However, bring sunscreen, remain hydrated, and be prepared for the heat.

Bruce Terry

Fall (September to November): Another popular time to visit Washington, D.C. is in the fall. In general, the weather is nice, with warm temperatures and low humidity.

The city is well-known for its stunning fall foliage, which provides a splash of color to the environment. September and October are especially pleasant, with temperatures ranging from 60°F (15°C) to 75°F (24°C). Furthermore, the crowds are lower than in the spring and summer, making it simpler to visit the city's attractions without feeling overwhelmed. The autumn season also provides opportunities to attend a variety of events and festivals, such as the H Street Festival and the National Book Festival.

Winter (December to February): Washington, D.C. experiences freezing weather and snowfall on occasion. The average temperature ranges from 30°F (-1°C) to 45°F (7°C), but wind chill can make it feel even colder. The benefit of traveling during this period is that there are fewer people and reduced hotel costs, making it an appealing option for budget-conscious travelers.

Some outdoor attractions, however, may have reduced hours or be closed for the season. Indoor attractions in the city, such as the Smithsonian museums, remain open and can be experienced without the typical throng. Additionally, the National Christmas Tree and seasonal decorations throughout the city contribute to the festive ambiance.

Bruce Terry

MONEY SAVING TIPS

Plan and Do Your Research: One of the most effective strategies to save money is to plan ahead of time. Determine the optimal time to visit Washington, D.C., taking into account both weather and peak visitor seasons. Look for special promotions on sights and activities, as well as cheap hotel prices and transportation.

Use Free Attractions: Washington, D.C. has a plethora of free attractions that allow you to tour the city without spending a thing. The National Mall, which contains prominent landmarks like the Lincoln Memorial and the Washington Monument, is completely free to view. The Smithsonian Museums, the United States Capitol Visitor Center, and the Library of Congress are among the prominent free attractions.

Invest in a Metro SmarTrip Card: Using public transportation to go around Washington, D.C. is a cost-effective option. Purchase a Metro SmarTrip Card, a reloadable fare card with lower rates than individual ticket sales. The card is valid on buses, Metrorail, and some regional trains, making it ideal for visiting the city and its surroundings.

Take Advantage of Free Walking Tours: Several groups in Washington, D.C. offer free walking tours that provide insightful information about the city's history, architecture, and culture. These tours, which are usually led by skilled guides, allow you to find hidden gems while saving money on guided tours.

Pack a Picnic: Rather than eating out every meal, save money by bringing a picnic lunch or snacks to enjoy in the city's magnificent parks or along the National Mall. There are numerous grocery stores and markets in the city where you can fill up on cheap and tasty food.

Explore Neighborhoods Outside of Downtown: While Washington, D.C.'s downtown region is full of notable buildings and attractions, try going into the city's neighborhoods for a more local experience. Georgetown, Adams Morgan, and Dupont Circle, for example, provide distinct stores, restaurants, and cultural activities without the exorbitant pricing seen in the city center.

Visit the Farmers' Markets: Washington, D.C. has a thriving farmers' market scene where you can buy fresh produce, regional delicacies, and inexpensive lunches. Visiting marketplaces such as Eastern Market and Union Market allows you to not only sample excellent food but also gain insight into the city's unique culture.

Discount passes, such as the Washington, D.C. Explorer Pass or the Go Washington, D.C. Card, should be considered. These cards provide cheap admission to a variety of sites and events, allowing you to save money while visiting the city's major attractions.

Bruce Terry

Look for Free Events and Festivals: Throughout the year, Washington, D.C. organizes several free events and festivals. Look through local event listings for free concerts, parades, cultural festivities, and other fascinating activities. These events allow you to immerse yourself in the colorful environment of the city while staying within your budget.

Look for Low-Cost Accommodations: While lodging prices can rapidly add up, there are ways to find low-cost solutions. Consider staying in hotels or hostels outside of the city center, where rates are typically lower. Additionally, look at alternative lodging options such as vacation rentals or guesthouses, which may provide better pricing and amenities than typical hotels.

Bruce Terry

WASHINGTON DC TRAVEL GUIDE 2023-2024

CHAPTER 3

GETTING AROUND WASHINGTON DC

Metrorail: One of the most popular modes of transportation in Washington, D.C. is the Metrorail system. It is made up of six color-coded lines that cover the city and its outskirts. Metrorail is well-known for its dependability, cleanliness, and vast network. It connects key sites such as the National Mall, the Smithsonian Museum, and the United States Capitol. Make sure to get a SmarTrip card, Metrorail's electronic fare card.

The Metrobus: system supplements the Metrorail system by providing bus services across the city. With over 300 routes, it is an economical and convenient way to access areas that are not served by the rail network. Buses have fare boxes that accept SmarTrip cards, cash, and smartphone payments.

DC Circulator: The DC Circulator is a popular bus service in Washington, D.C. that is specifically tailored for visitors and commuters. It has six unique routes that connect important tourist destinations such as Georgetown, the National Mall, and Union Station. The buses stop every ten minutes, making it an efficient method to tour the city.

Capital Bikeshare: Capital Bikeshare is a large bike-sharing program in Washington, D.C. Visitors can rent a bike for a short amount of time from hundreds of stations located throughout the city. Find a station, pay with a credit card, and begin pedaling. This environmentally friendly option offers more flexible mobility, particularly in locations with bike lanes and trails.

Taxis and Ride-Sharing: Taxis can be hailed on the street or found at designated taxi stops throughout Washington, D.C. Furthermore, ride-sharing services such as Uber and Lyft are popular in the city, providing a handy and frequently cost-effective mode of transportation. Simply download the appropriate app, request a ride, and wait for your driver.

Rental automobiles: Rental automobiles are widely accessible in Washington, D.C. for individuals who prefer the independence of driving alone. However, it is important to note that traffic and parking might be difficult, especially in congested downtown districts. If you do decide to rent a car, learn about parking restrictions and consider parking in a garage or at on-street parking meters.

Walking: Washington, D.C., especially in the downtown area, is a very walkable city. Many of the city's biggest attractions, such as the White House, Smithsonian museums, and memorials, are easily accessible by foot. Walking allows you to immerse yourself in the dynamic ambiance of the city while also discovering hidden gems along the route.

Electric Scooters: In recent years, electric scooters have gained appeal as a fun and effective way to navigate around the city. Companies such as Lime, Bird, and Spin rent out dockless electric scooters via smartphone apps. However, make sure you are informed of local rules and ride sensibly, adhering to traffic laws and safety guidelines.

Hop-on-hop-off tour buses are a wonderful alternative whether you're visiting Washington, D.C. for the first time or want to experience the city's highlights with a guided tour. These buses travel along predetermined itineraries and allow visitors to board and disembark at various locations. The narrated tours enlighten visitors about the city's history and landmarks.

Water Taxis: Consider taking a water taxi for a unique and scenic way to travel in Washington, D.C. The Potomac River is navigable, and multiple firms provide water taxi services connecting major waterfront attractions such as Georgetown, National Harbor, and Old Town Alexandria. During your water taxi ride, take in stunning views of the city's skyline and prominent sites.

Bruce Terry

HOW TO GET FROM WASHINGTON DC AIRPORT TO CITY CENTER

Distance from Washington Dulles International Airport (IAD) to the City Center:

Dulles International Airport, located approximately 26 miles west of downtown Washington DC, provides many transportation alternatives to the city center:

Metrorail Silver Line: The Silver Line Express Bus connects Dulles International Airport to the Wiehle-Reston East Metrorail Station. You can then take the Metrorail right to the city center. Take the following steps:

Look for the "Ground Transportation" signage as you exit the airport and proceed to curb 2E or 2F.

Board the Silver Line Express Bus (Route 5A) and pay with a fare card or a contactless payment option.

Arrive at Wiehle-Reston East Station and transfer to the Metrorail Silver Line, which will take you to Largo Town Center.

Disembark at your preferred city center station, such as Metro Center, Gallery Place-Chinatown, or Union Station.

Bruce Terry

Taxis and shared shuttles: Dulles Airport has a plethora of shared shuttle services and taxis that provide door-to-door service to the city core. Outside the arrivals area, look for the designated shuttle or taxi stands. Make careful to ask about fares and select a reliable supplier.

The distance from Ronald Reagan Washington National Airport (DCA) to City Center is:

Ronald Reagan Washington National Airport is the nearest airport to downtown Washington DC, located just across the Potomac River. Here are some choices for transportation:

Metrorail: Reagan National Airport is directly connected to the Metrorail system, giving it a great option for getting to the city center. Take the following steps:

When you arrive, follow the signs to the airport's Metrorail station, which is located between Terminals B and C.

Buy a fare card or make a contactless payment.

Depending on your destination, take the Metrorail Yellow or Blue Line.

Disembark at your preferred city center station, such as Metro Center, Gallery Place-Chinatown, or Union Station.

Bruce Terry

Taxis, ride-sharing services, and shuttles: At DCA, taxis, rideshare services such as Uber and Lyft, and shared buses are easily available. Simply follow the signs outside the airport terminals to the ground transportation area or designated pickup zones. Confirm the fares and select the best alternative for your needs.

BWI Airport to City Center: While BWI Airport is approximately 32 miles northeast of downtown Washington DC, it is still a feasible alternative for reaching the city center. Consider the following modes of transportation:

MARC Train: The MARC Train connects BWI Airport to Washington DC's Union Station, providing a cost-effective and efficient transportation option. What you must do is as follows:

Take the signs to the BWI Airport MARC/Amtrak Station, which is located next to the airport.

Purchase a ticket at the ticket vending machine at the station or use a contactless payment option.

Board a MARC Penn Line train bound for Union Station.

Depart from Union Station, which is conveniently placed in the heart of the city.

Shuttles and Taxis: Shared shuttles and taxis are available outside the BWI Airport arrivals area. Look for the approved pick-up

Bruce Terry

locations or ask airport personnel for assistance. It is best to check prices and select a reliable service provider.

HOW TO GET FROM WASHINGTON DC AIRPORT TO THE NEAREST HOTELS

Ronald Reagan Washington National Airport (DCA): Located just across the Potomac River from downtown Washington D.C., Ronald Reagan Washington National Airport is a popular choice for visitors to the nation's capital.

a. *Taxi/Cab:* Taking a taxi or cab from the airport is one of the most convenient solutions. Taxis are widely accessible outside the terminal, and the travel to most downtown hotels takes between 10 and 20 minutes, depending on traffic. Use licensed taxis and confirm the estimated rate before entering.

b. *Ride-Hailing Services:* Popular ride-hailing services such as Uber and Lyft are available at DCA. Simply schedule a ride using the corresponding app on your smartphone, and your driver will meet you outside the terminal at the authorized ride-sharing pickup area. The app provides fare estimations as well as alternatives for shared or private journeys.

c. *Metro:* The Washington Metropolitan Area Transit Authority (WMATA) runs a Metro station at the airport, aptly known as the "Ronald Reagan Washington National Airport" station. The Blue and Yellow lines service the airport. To pay for your travel, you can buy a fare card at the station or use a contactless payment option. Check the Metro map to see which station is closest to your accommodation and plan your itinerary appropriately.

d. *Shuttle Services:* Some hotels near DCA provide complimentary airport shuttle service. It is best to contact your hotel ahead of time to enquire about availability and schedule. Look for signage or ask airport staff for directions to the authorized shuttle pickup spot.

IAD, or Washington Dulles International Airport, is in Dulles, Virginia, some 26 miles west of the capital. It handles domestic as well as foreign flights.

a. *Taxi/Cab:* Taxis are accessible outside the airport terminal in the ground transportation area. The travel time to downtown hotels might range from 45 minutes to more than an hour depending on traffic conditions. Use licensed taxis and agree on a fare before beginning your journey.

b. *Ride-Sharing Services:* Dulles Airport offers Uber, Lyft, and other ride-sharing services. Book a ride through the app, and your driver will meet you outside the terminal at the designated ride-sharing pickup area. The app will provide fare estimates and ride possibilities.

c. *Washington Flyer Silver Line Express Bus:* The Washington Flyer Silver Line Express Bus connects Dulles International Airport to the Wiehle-Reston East Metro station. Transfer to the Silver Line Metro and continue your journey to downtown Washington, D.C., or the nearest Metro-accessible hotel. The bus leaves from the airport's Ground Transportation Level.

d. *Shuttle Services:* Some hotels near Dulles International Airport provide shuttle services to their customers. Contact your hotel ahead of time to see whether they offer a shuttle service and to inquire about pickup locations and schedules.

Baltimore/Washington International Thurgood Marshall Airport (BWI):

Baltimore/Washington International Thurgood Marshall Airport is located in Linthicum, Maryland, approximately 32 miles northeast of downtown Washington, D.C. While it is not as close to the city center as the other two airports, it is nevertheless an alternative for visitors to Washington, D.C.

a. *Taxi/Cab:* Taxis are readily available outside the airport terminal at the taxi stop. Depending on traffic, the journey time to downtown hotels might range from 45 minutes to more than an hour. Before beginning your journey, choose licensed taxis and discuss the fee.

Bruce Terry

b. *Ride-Sharing Services:* At BWI Airport, Uber, Lyft, and other ride-sharing services are available. When you book a ride through the app, your driver will meet you at the appropriate ride-sharing pickup location. The app will provide fare estimations and ride possibilities.

c. *MARC Train:* The Penn Line of the MARC Train connects BWI Airport to Union Station in downtown Washington, D.C. The railway station is approximately one mile from the airport, and a free shuttle service, labeled "MARC/Amtrak Shuttle," is provided to take passengers between the airport and the train station. Once at Union Station, you may easily reach downtown hotels via Metro or other modes of transportation.

d. *Shuttle Services:* Some BWI Airport hotels offer shuttle services to their clients. Inquire with your hotel ahead of time about availability, pickup locations, and scheduling.

PUBLIC WIFI AVAILABILITY IN WASHINGTON DC

Public WiFi Hotspots in Popular Tourist Areas: Washington, D.C. understands the value of providing residents and visitors with reliable internet access. As a result, many famous tourist destinations now have public WiFi stations. Here are some key areas where public WiFi can be found:

Bruce Terry

a. *National Mall:* The National Mall, which includes prominent structures such as the Washington Monument and the Lincoln Memorial, provides free WiFi throughout the park. While visiting the region, visitors can easily connect to the "Smithsonian Visitor" network and enjoy seamless internet access.

b. *Museums and Monuments:* Free WiFi is available at many museums and monuments in Washington, D.C., including the Smithsonian museums, the National Gallery of Art, and the Holocaust Memorial Museum. Look for network names such as "SmithsonianWiFi" or "GalleryWiFi" to join.

c. *Parks and Recreational Places:* The city's parks and recreational places, such as Dupont Circle and Georgetown Waterfront Park, offer free public WiFi. These hotspots allow visitors to rest outside while remaining connected.

d. *Libraries:* All branches of the District of Columbia Public Library system have free WiFi. Libraries might be a wonderful option if you need a quiet place to work or catch up on your internetwork.

Public WiFi in transit Hubs: Washington, D.C. has a comprehensive public transit system, and WiFi connectivity is offered in a variety of transportation hubs, including:

a. *Washington Metropolitan Area Transit Authority (WMATA):* The Metro, the city's subway system, provides free WiFi in most of its stations. While waiting for a train, commuters and visitors can connect to the "Metro-Public" network to access the internet.

b. *Union Station:* Union Station, a key transportation hub in Washington, D.C., offers free WiFi throughout the building. You may stay connected to the internet while waiting for a train or visiting the stores and eateries.

Additional WiFi choices: In addition to public WiFi hotspots, there are several other choices for internet connection in Washington, D.C. to consider:

Coffee Houses and Restaurants: Many cafes, restaurants, and fast-food restaurants in the city provide free WiFi to consumers. You can stay connected while drinking coffee or eating a meal.

a. *Hotels & Lodging:* Most hotels in Washington, D.C. offer WiFi to their visitors. It's a good idea to check with your lodging provider about WiFi availability and any potential fees.

CHAPTER 4

WHAT YOU NEED TO PACK ON A TRIP TO WASHINGTON DC

• WHAT TO PACK FOR WINTER

Warm Clothing:

Winter in Washington, D.C. may be fairly cold, with temperatures ranging from below-freezing to moderate. Therefore, carrying warm clothing is crucial. Consider the following items:

a. *Coats and Jackets:* Bring a large winter coat or a warm jacket with a hood to protect yourself from the chilly winds. Opt for down-filled or insulated alternatives for ultimate warmth.

b. *Sweaters and Sweatshirts:* Pack a range of sweaters and sweatshirts made of wool or fleece for layering. These will provide extra insulation and can be readily added or withdrawn depending on the temperature.

c. *Long-sleeved Shirts and Turtlenecks:* Include multiple long-sleeved shirts and turtlenecks to wear as base layers under your sweaters or jackets. These will assist trap heat and keep you warm.

d. *Thermal Underwear:* Consider carrying thermal underwear or long johns to wear beneath your pants. These will provide an additional layer of warmth and insulation.

e. *Hats, Gloves, and Scarves:* Don't forget to carry a warm cap, gloves, and a scarf to protect your extremities from the stinging cold. Look for choices made of wool or fleece to provide higher insulation.

Footwear:

Choosing the appropriate footwear is vital for walking in Washington, D.C. during winter. Here are some recommendations:

a. *Insulated Boots:* Pack a pair of robust and waterproof insulated boots with adequate traction to negotiate snowy or icy situations. Look for alternatives that are designed to keep your feet toasty in cold climates.

b. *Thick Socks:* Bring several pairs of thick, moisture-wicking socks made of wool or synthetic materials. These will keep your feet warm and dry during your outdoor activities.

Bottoms:

When it comes to bottoms, consider the following:

a. *Pants and Jeans*: Pack a few pairs of thick slacks or jeans made of hefty materials to keep your legs toasty. Avoid light textiles that won't give appropriate insulation.

b. *Leggings or Thermal Tights:* If you intend on wearing skirts or dresses, pack a few pairs of thermal leggings or tights to wear underneath for added warmth.

Items: In addition to apparel, there are a few crucial items to consider:

a. *Backpack or Bag:* Bring a durable backpack or bag to carry your needs, including water, snacks, and extra clothing. Make sure it is robust and has enough room to fit your items.

b. *Hand Warmers:* Consider taking hand warmers to give quick heat to your hands during particularly chilly days or when spending extended periods outside.

c. *Portable Charger:* Cold weather can drain your smartphone's battery quickly. Carry a portable charger to ensure your devices stay powered up, especially if you're dependent on maps or travel apps.

• WHAT TO PACK FOR SPRING

Spring in Washington, D.C. is distinguished by warm temperatures and changeable weather conditions. Temperatures can fluctuate from 50 to 75 degrees Fahrenheit (10 to 24 degrees Celsius), so be prepared for both cool and warm days. However, it's vital to remember that spring might also bring rain showers, so wear rain gear.

Bruce Terry

a. *Layers:* Because the weather can be unpredictable, layering is essential. Pack lightweight, breathable clothing items that can be easily layered with a sweater or light jacket, such as t-shirts, blouses, and button-down shirts.

b. *Jacket or Coat:* For chilly mornings and evenings, bring a light jacket or coat. To stay dry during spring showers, choose a waterproof or water-resistant choice.

c. *Pants and Skirts:* For adaptability, bring a combination of long pants and skirts. Jeans or trousers are appropriate for most occasions, whereas skirts or dresses are appropriate for formal or special occasions.

d. *Comfortable Shoes*: Pack comfortable walking shoes for extended hikes and touring the city. Shoes with good support, such as sneakers, flats, or sandals, are appropriate.

e. *Accessories:* Remember to bring a wide-brimmed hat or cap to shield yourself from the sun, as well as sunglasses and sunscreen.

Rain Gear:

Springtime in Washington, D.C. can bring sporadic rain showers, so be prepared.

a. *Umbrella:* Bring a small, lightweight umbrella that fits easily into your bag. It will be useful during sudden rain storms.

b. *Raincoat or Poncho*: While visiting the city, a waterproof raincoat or poncho will keep you dry. To be comfortable, choose a breathable option.

c. *Backpack:* Bring a comfortable backpack to carry basics such as a water bottle, snacks, camera, guidebook, and maps on your sightseeing adventures.

d. *Comfortable Day Pack:* If you plan to explore the city's prominent landmarks and parks, bring a comfortable day pack with you to carry your needs, such as water, food, and extra layers of clothes.

e. *Binoculars:* Because Washington, D.C. has so many parks and wildlife places, binoculars are an excellent tool for seeing birds and other wildlife.

f. *Camera:* Use a camera or a smartphone with a camera to capture the splendor of spring in Washington, D.C.

Cultural and Formal Apparel:

a. *Formal Attire:* Pack appropriate formal apparel such as a dress or suit if you want to attend formal events, concerts, or dining at expensive businesses.

b. *Business Casual Attire:* Bring business casual clothing options such as trousers, blazers, and collared shirts or blouses to business meetings or more formal occasions.

Bruce Terry

Miscellaneous Items:

a. *Electrical Adapters:* Bring a suitable adaptor to charge your electronics if you are traveling from a nation with a different electrical outlet system.

b. *Portable Charger:* Bring a portable charger for your electronic gadgets to guarantee you stay connected throughout the day.

c. *Travel Guides and Maps:* Bring travel guides or maps of Washington, D.b. with you to help you explore the city and organize your activities.

d. *Medications:* If you require prescription medications, make sure you carry enough for the duration of your vacation.

• WHAT TO PACK FOR SUMMER

Lightweight Clothing: Summers in Washington, D.C. are hot and humid, so bring lightweight and breathable clothing. Pack the following items:

T-shirts and tank tops: Choose light, moisture-wicking fabrics like cotton or linen.

Shorts and Skirts: To beat the summer heat, bring a couple of pairs of comfy shorts or skirts.

Sundresses and lightweight trousers: For more formal occasions or cooler evenings, include a few sundresses or lightweight slacks.

Bruce Terry

Light layers: Even though the days are hot, the evenings can be cool. For such occasions, bring a light jumper or cardigan.

Comfortable footwear:

Expect to do a lot of walking in Washington, D.C., so bring comfortable shoes. Pack the following items:

Walking Shoes: Bring a comfortable pair of walking shoes or sneakers to explore the city's many attractions.

Sandals: For warmer days or casual outings, bring a pair of comfy sandals.

Dress Shoes: Bring a pair of dress shoes if you want to visit fancy restaurants or attend formal events.

Sun Protection:

Because the summer sun may be fierce in Washington, D.C., it's critical to protect yourself from damaging UV rays. Remember to bring the following items:

Sunscreen: To protect your skin from sunburn, carry a broad-spectrum sunscreen with a high SPF.

Sunglasses: Bring sunglasses to protect your eyes from the harsh sun.

Bruce Terry

Pack a wide-brimmed hat or a baseball cap to keep your face and head protected.

Rain Gear:

During the summer, Washington, D.C. experiences sporadic showers. To be ready, pack the following items:

Lightweight Rain Jacket or Poncho: Bring a waterproof and breathable jacket or poncho with you to keep you dry during unexpected showers.

Compact Umbrella: Bring a compact, foldable umbrella with you for convenient storage and quick rain protection.

Consider carrying the following items to make your visit more convenient and enjoyable:

Bring a lightweight backpack or day bag to carry basics like water bottles, snacks, a camera, and a guidebook.

Reusable Water Bottle*:*

Keep hydrated by carrying a reusable water bottle, as staying hydrated is critical in the summer heat.

Power Bank: A portable power bank will keep your electrical devices charged throughout the day.

Bruce Terry

Travel adaptor: Bring a travel adaptor with you if you're traveling from outside the United States.

WHAT TO PACK FOR AUTUMN

Layered clothes: Because autumn in Washington, D.C. may bring varying temperatures, it's essential to carry layered clothes to adapt to shifting weather conditions. Long-sleeved shirts, lightweight sweaters, cardigans, and a medium-weight jacket are all appropriate. Layering enables you to add or remove garments as required during the day, guaranteeing comfort in a variety of climates.

Comfortable Footwear: Because Washington, D.C. is best explored on foot, bringing comfortable footwear is ideal for extended walks. Choose closed-toe shoes or sneakers with sufficient support and cushioning. Check the weather forecast before your journey to see whether you'll need waterproof shoes or boots in the event of rain.

Rain Jacket: Autumn in Washington, D.C. might be accompanied by rain. Pack a small umbrella or a waterproof jacket to keep dry and continue visiting the city even if it rains. Being prepared for unforeseen weather changes is usually a smart idea.

Scarves, hats, and gloves: As the season develops, temperatures in Washington, D.C. may begin to fall. Pack scarves, hats, and gloves to keep you warm and comfy in the mornings and nights. These

Bruce Terry

accessories not only keep you warm but also offer a fashionable touch to your attire.

Bottoms with Versatility: When it comes to bottoms, pack selections that can be combined and matched with a variety of tops. Include neutral-colored jeans, trousers, or skirts that may be dressed up or down depending on the occasion. Consider carrying leggings or thermal pants for added warmth on cooler days.

A comfortable daypack is a must-have for touring Washington, D.C. It lets you carry necessities such as a water bottle, food, a camera, and a guidebook. To guarantee a pleasant experience while you visit the city's myriad attractions, look for a lightweight and comfortable daypack that distributes weight evenly.

Important Travel Documents and Necessities: Don't forget to pack your passport, identification, and any applicable visas. Pack a travel adaptor for charging your electrical gadgets, as well as a portable charger to keep your phone charged all day.

Binoculars and camera: Washington, D.C. is home to renowned sites and beautiful views. Pack a high-quality camera and additional memory cards to record these priceless moments. Binoculars are also useful for taking a closer look at faraway landmarks such as the Washington Monument or the United States Capitol.

Bruce Terry

CHAPTER 5

TOP TOURIST DESTINATIONS IN WASHINGTON DC

The National Mall: The National Mall is a large park running from the Capitol Building to the Lincoln Memorial. It is home to notable monuments such as the Washington Monument, the Lincoln Memorial, and the Vietnam Veterans Memorial. Visitors may wander around the Reflecting Pool and take in the breathtaking vistas of the monuments that pay honor to the nation's past and its great leaders.

The White House: No journey to Washington, D.C. is complete without a stop at the White House, the official house and workplace of the President of the United States. While tours of the inside are restricted, tourists may still enjoy the neoclassical architecture and explore the adjacent Lafayette Square.

Smithsonian Institution: The Smithsonian Institution is a world-renowned network of museums and research institutions. It comprises 17 museums and galleries, such as the National Air and Space Museum, the National Museum of Natural History, and the National Museum of American History. These organizations hold extensive collections of art, artifacts, and exhibitions that give

Bruce Terry

insights into diverse elements of American history, culture, and science.

U.S. Capitol and Capitol Hill: The U.S. Capitol, the seat of the United States Congress, is an architectural wonder and a symbol of democracy. Visitors may enjoy guided tours of the ancient building to learn about its history, art, and legislative process. Nearby, Capitol Hill is a delightful area with gorgeous rowhouses, fashionable boutiques, and a thriving food scene.

The Library of Congress: The Library of Congress is the biggest in the world, storing millions of books, manuscripts, photos, and maps. Visitors may tour its exquisite reading rooms, appreciate its spectacular architecture, and even study rare historical documents, like the Gutenberg Bible and the original copy of the Declaration of Independence.

National Gallery of Art: Art fans will be intrigued by the National Gallery of Art, which contains an impressive collection of European and American masterpieces. From Renaissance paintings to Impressionist works, the museum shows important items by artists such as Leonardo da Vinci, Rembrandt, Monet, and Van Gogh. The sculpture park, with its outdoor installations, is a quiet refuge in the center of the city.

Bruce Terry

Georgetown: One of Washington, D.C.'s oldest districts, Georgetown provides a lovely blend of history, shopping, and food. Visitors may meander through cobblestone streets surrounded by ancient residences, discover fashionable stores, and enjoy exquisite food at the waterfront restaurants along the historic C&O Canal.

National Zoo: The National Zoo, part of the Smithsonian Institution, is a favored location for families. Located in Rock Creek Park, the zoo is home to more than 2,000 species, including giant pandas, elephants, lions, and gorillas. Visitors may enjoy informative displays, and animal presentations, and perhaps get a peek at the cute panda babies.

Arlington National Cemetery: Located just across the Potomac River in Virginia, Arlington National Cemetery is a serious and melancholy visit. It serves as the last resting place for more than 400,000 military servicemen and their families. Visitors may observe the Changing of the Guard ritual at the Tomb of the Unknown Soldier and pay their respects to fallen soldiers.

The Kennedy Center: The John F. Kennedy Center for the Performing Arts is a cultural center that offers a broad variety of productions, including theater, ballet, symphonic concerts, and opera. Visitors may watch world-class shows at its numerous theaters and take in the panoramic views of the city from the rooftop terrace.

Bruce Terry

WASHINGTON DC TRAVEL GUIDE 2023-2024

CHAPTER 6

BEST RESTAURANTS IN WASHINGTON DC

The Inn at Little Washington: Nestled in the charming town of Washington, Virginia, only a short drive from D.C., The Inn at Little Washington is a world-renowned culinary destination. This three-Michelin-starred restaurant, directed by Chef Patrick O'Connell, delivers an outstanding dining experience. The menu offers expertly made meals employing locally sourced ingredients, with novel taste combinations and outstanding presentation. The beautiful dining rooms and outstanding service create an environment of refined luxury, making The Inn at Little Washington a must-visit for any culinary connoisseur.

Pineapple and Pearls: Located on Capitol Hill, Pineapple and Pearls is a Michelin two-starred restaurant recognized for its outstanding tasting menus. The culinary team, led by Chef Aaron Silverman, delivers an innovative and ever-changing array of meals that showcase seasonal ingredients. The restaurant provides both a la carte and prix fixe menus, guaranteeing a customized experience. With its modern but warm ambiance and dedicated service, Pineapple and Pearls assure a delightful dining encounter.

Fiola Mare: For seafood lovers, Fiola Mare is an amazing option. Situated near the Georgetown waterfront, this premium Italian seafood restaurant provides stunning views of the Potomac River.

Bruce Terry

The cuisine, selected by Chef Fabio Trabocchi, provides a broad range of fresh seafood, including oysters, crudo, and entire fish dishes. The exquisite atmosphere, kind hospitality, and well-crafted wine selection make Fiola Mare a wonderful setting for a romantic meal or special event.

Rose's Luxury: Known for its fun and imaginative food, Rose's Luxury has become a favorite eating destination in the Barracks Row area. Led by Chef Aaron Silverman, this Michelin-starred restaurant provides a distinctive cuisine that mixes world tastes with a touch of whimsy. Diners may anticipate meals such as pig sausage, habanero, and lychee salad or popcorn soup with lobster and Thai basil. The restaurant's relaxing environment, communal seating, and superb service add to its welcome and convivial mood.

Maydan: Maydan takes tourists on a gastronomic voyage across the Middle East and North Africa. Located in the U Street Corridor, this bustling restaurant provides an engaging dining experience. The open-fire cooking methods and fragrant spices generate powerful and intriguing tastes in meals like entire roasted lamb shoulder and wood-fired bread. The restaurant's décor, filled with unique designs, transports customers to a Moroccan-inspired paradise. The communal eating layout and dynamic environment add to the conviviality of the dining experience at Maydan.

Bruce Terry

BUDGET-FRIENDLY HOTELS IN WASHINGTON DC

The George Washington University Inn: Located in the Foggy Bottom district, The George Washington University Inn is a pleasant and economical hotel suited for budget visitors. The hotel provides clean and comfortable rooms with contemporary conveniences such as flat-screen TVs, free Wi-Fi, and coffee machines. The handy location gives easy access to major sights including the White House and the Lincoln Memorial. Additionally, complimentary breakfast is provided, offering a terrific start to your day without additional expense.

Hampton Inn Washington, D.C./White House: Just a few streets away from the White House, the Hampton Inn Washington, D.C./White House provides moderate prices without sacrificing quality. The hotel has large and well-appointed rooms with services including free Wi-Fi, flat-screen TVs, and mini-refrigerators. Guests may enjoy a free cooked breakfast to fuel their day of touring the city. The hotel's central position gives easy access to major attractions, museums, and culinary choices.

Holiday Inn Washington-Capitol: Situated near the National Mall, the Holiday Inn Washington-Capitol provides pleasant and economical lodgings for budget-conscious guests. The hotel has contemporary and large rooms equipped with comforts like flat-screen TVs, mini-fridges, and work tables. Guests may relax in the on-site fitness facility or enjoy a meal at the hotel's restaurant. The hotel's closeness to prominent monuments including the Capitol Building and Smithsonian institution's makes it a good option for budget tourists.

The Normandy Hotel: Nestled in the picturesque Dupont Circle district, The Normandy Hotel is a boutique hotel that delivers an economical and distinctive overnight experience. The rooms include a combination of contemporary conveniences and traditional design, giving a pleasant and welcoming ambiance. Guests may enjoy a free continental breakfast and make use of the hotel's fitness facility. The location gives easy access to Dupont Circle's busy food scene and is within walking distance to the Metro, offering simple transfer to other areas of the city.

Hotel Hive: Hotel Hive, situated in the Foggy Bottom district, provides a modern and budget-friendly choice for guests seeking a distinctive experience. The hotel has economically built rooms inspired by the notion of beehives, optimizing space and utility. Each room is outfitted with contemporary facilities including flat-screen TVs, Wi-Fi, and in-room safes. The hotel also features a rooftop bar and lounge, giving a picturesque area to relax and enjoy the city views. The ideal location gives quick access to attractions like the Kennedy Center and the National Mall.

Bruce Terry

BEST LUXURY HOTELS IN WASHINGTON DC

The Jefferson, Washington, D.C.: The Jefferson is a historic luxury hotel situated only four blocks from the White House. Combining traditional elegance with contemporary comforts, this five-star hotel provides spacious rooms and suites furnished with antique antiques, soft bedding, and marble baths. Guests may enjoy extraordinary dining experiences at the Michelin-starred Plume restaurant or relax at the stylish Quill Bar, noted for its enormous whiskey collection. The Jefferson also includes a quiet spa, fitness center, and individual concierge services, assuring an enjoyable stay.

The Watergate Hotel: Situated on the banks of the Potomac River, The Watergate Hotel is an iconic building that has been expertly rebuilt to give a modern luxury experience. Its elegant rooms and suites include contemporary design, floor-to-ceiling windows, and panoramic views of the city. The hotel's rooftop bar and lounge, Top of the Gate, give a wonderful venue to sip creative cocktails while taking in the amazing views of Washington, D.C. Other features include a magnificent spa, a state-of-the-art fitness facility, and world-class dining selections.

The Hay-Adams: Located steps away from the White House, The Hay-Adams is a historic hotel famous for its exquisite elegance and superb service. Offering spectacular views of the city's monuments, including the Washington Monument and the National Mall, this elegant facility has spacious guest rooms and suites furnished with custom-designed furniture, Italian marble baths, and contemporary conveniences. The Hay-Adams also has two award-winning restaurants, The Lafayette and Off the Record, noted for their outstanding food and beautiful setting.

The Four Seasons Hotel Washington, D.C.: Renowned for its outstanding service and attention to detail, The Four Seasons Hotel Washington, D.C. provides a magnificent getaway in the heart of the city's historic Georgetown area. With large rooms and suites with modern décor and spectacular city views, visitors can anticipate the highest comfort and luxury. The hotel has an exceptional spa, an indoor pool, and a fitness center. Dining choices include the Michelin-starred Bourbon Steak restaurant, where visitors may experience wonderful cuts of meat and superb wines.

The St. Regis Washington, D.C.: Situated only two blocks from the White House, St. Regis Washington, D.C. symbolizes ageless grandeur and refinement. The hotel's nicely designed rooms and suites offer high ceilings, unique furniture, and marble baths. Guests may luxuriate in the hotel's great dining experiences, such as the famed Decanter wine bar and the Astor Terrace, providing al fresco dining. St. Regis also provides individual butler service, a state-of-the-art fitness facility, and a quiet spa, assuring an exquisite stay.

Bruce Terry

BEST SHOPPING MALLS IN WASHINGTON DC

CityCenterDC: Located in the center of downtown Washington, DC, CityCenterDC stands out as a great retail destination. This upmarket mall provides a combination of high-end international brands, luxury shops, and great eating choices. With its modern architecture and exquisite ambiance, CityCenterDC provides a luxury shopping experience. Shoppers may discover known fashion labels like Gucci, Louis Vuitton, and Hermes, as well as specialty beauty and lifestyle businesses. Additionally, the mall organizes many cultural events and art exhibits, making it a dynamic nexus for fashion, art, and entertainment.

Tysons Corner Center: Situated just outside Washington, DC, in McLean, Virginia, Tysons Corner Center is one of the biggest and most popular shopping malls in the area. Boasting over 300 retailers, this enormous mall caters to any shopper's demands.

From flagship shops of recognized companies like Nordstrom and Macy's to specialist businesses presenting the newest fashion trends, Tysons Corner Center provides a varied selection of shopping alternatives. The mall also contains an amazing food court and expensive restaurants, so tourists can indulge in wonderful meals after a long day of shopping.

Pentagon City Mall: Located conveniently between the Pentagon and Reagan National Airport, Pentagon City Mall is a favorite

Bruce Terry

shopping destination for both residents and visitors. This multi-level shopping mall has a vast selection of retailers, ranging from well-known fashion brands to electronics and home items. Pentagon City Mall is centered on major department shops like Nordstrom and Macy's, giving a full shopping experience. The mall also provides a range of culinary choices, making it a wonderful spot to unwind and refuel throughout your shopping binge.

Union Market: For those seeking a distinctive and stylish shopping experience, Union Market is a must-visit place. Located in the lively NoMa district of Washington, DC, this busy marketplace exhibits a handpicked variety of local vendors, craftsmen, and independent businesses. Union Market is noted for its thriving food scene, providing a varied selection of gastronomic pleasures, including gourmet nibbles, handcrafted chocolates, and exotic cuisines. Beyond food, tourists may browse boutique stores specialized in fashion, home décor, and handcrafted crafts, making Union Market a great spot to uncover one-of-a-kind treasures.

The Wharf: Situated along the gorgeous Potomac River, The Wharf is a waterfront attraction that blends shopping, eating, and entertainment. This bustling sector contains a mix of contemporary retail shops, luxury boutiques, and specialty retailers. The Wharf's distinctive boardwalk ambiance and spectacular waterfront vistas make it a lovely setting for customers. Visitors may visit a selection of stores selling apparel, accessories, home décor, and more. Additionally, The Wharf has frequent live concerts, festivals, and outdoor events, making it a fantastic destination to spend a day indulging in retail therapy and enjoying the busy waterfront atmosphere.

BEST MUSEUMS IN WASHINGTON DC

National Museum of American History: The National Museum of American History is a must-visit location for individuals interested in the history and culture of the United States.

The museum shows a huge collection of items, ranging from the Star-Spangled Banner and the actual flag that inspired the national song to the famed ruby slippers from From "The Wizard of Oz." Through engaging exhibits, multimedia presentations, and interesting displays that highlight significant occasions, well-known figures, and everyday life in America, visitors may fully immerse themselves in the history of the nation.

National Air and Space Museum: For aviation and space aficionados, the National Air and Space Museum is an outstanding must-see. This museum, part of the Smithsonian Institution, holds the biggest collection of vintage aircraft and spacecraft in the world. Visitors may gaze at historic items such as the Wright Brothers' 1903 Flyer, the Apollo 11 Command Module, and the Spirit of St. Louis. The museum also includes interactive displays, flight simulators, and educational programs that give insight into the mysteries of aeronautical exploration.

National Gallery of Art: Art aficionados will be attracted by the National Gallery of Art, home to a vast collection of paintings, sculptures, and decorative arts spanning centuries. The museum contains treasures by notable painters including Leonardo da Vinci, Vincent van Gogh, and Pablo Picasso. Visitors may study numerous art movements, from the Renaissance through Impressionism and beyond, while also enjoying special exhibits and interesting educational activities. The quiet sculpture garden provides a serene outdoor spot to relax and examine intriguing artworks.

Smithsonian National Museum of Natural History: The Smithsonian National Museum of Natural History is a treasure mine of information, encouraging visitors to experience the marvels of the natural world. The museum's huge collection comprises millions of objects, including dinosaur fossils, jewels, and ancient artifacts. The Hall of Human Origins examines our evolutionary past, while the Butterfly Pavilion enables visitors to view and learn about these fragile insects up close. The interactive Q? rius Learning Space provides hands-on activities and educational events that engage guests of all ages.

Bruce Terry

United States Holocaust Memorial Museum: A visit to the United States Holocaust Memorial Museum is a somber and highly affecting experience. This museum acts as a living monument to the victims of the Holocaust, attempting to educate visitors about the history and repercussions of genocide. Through dramatic exhibitions, personal testimony, and multimedia presentations, the museum chronicles the experiences of those impacted by this sad chapter in human history. Visitors may obtain a comprehensive knowledge of the Holocaust's effect and the significance of supporting tolerance, human rights, and social justice.

BEST PARKS AND GARDENS IN WASHINGTON DC

The National Mall and Memorial Parks: The National Mall, which stretches from the United States Capitol to the Lincoln Memorial, is an important historical and cultural hub in Washington, D.C. It includes the Washington Monument, the World War II Memorial, and the Vietnam Veterans Memorial, among others. The National Mall's immense green expanse gives plenty of area for picnics, outdoor activities, and events. This park's meticulously kept flowers and fountains add to its attractiveness, making it a must-see location.

The United States Botanic Garden: is a live plant museum that demonstrates the beauty and variety of the world's flora. This 3-acre garden near the Capitol offers a variety of themed gardens, including

Bruce Terry

the Rose Garden, Medicinal Plants Garden, and the First Ladies Water Garden. Visitors may take guided tours, see educational displays, and explore the conservatory, which is home to exotic plants from several habitats. The United States Botanic Garden is not only a beautiful site, but it also acts as a resource for sustainable gardening methods.

Rock Creek Park: Rock Creek Park is a 2,000-acre natural refuge in the center of Washington, D.C. This urban park provides a variety of leisure opportunities, including hiking paths, equestrian riding, and bicycle routes. Visitors may enjoy the park's picturesque splendor while visiting historical monuments such as the Pierce Mill and the Old Stone House. Rock Creek Park also offers birding and wildlife photography possibilities, making it a refuge for outdoor enthusiasts and environment lovers.

Dumbarton Oaks: This ancient mansion in Georgetown is known for its beautiful grounds and rich history. The gardens' exquisite design incorporates aspects of Italian, French, and English landscaping techniques. Visitors may meander through the exquisite terraced gardens, enjoy the stunning sculptures, and unwind by the tranquil fountains. Dumbarton Oaks also holds art exhibits, concerts, and talks, all of which contribute to its cultural relevance.

Meridian Hill Park: commonly known as Malcolm X Park, is a popular meeting place and cultural center in Washington, D.C. A flowing fountain in the center of the park is encircled by tiered gardens and shaded trees. It provides a tranquil setting for picnics, yoga sessions, and community gatherings. Meridian Hill Park is well-known for its Sunday drum circles when musicians get together to create a lively and dynamic atmosphere. The park's setting amid the varied Adams Morgan neighborhood adds to its allure, giving it a real reflection of the city's colorful personality.

BEST NIGHTCLUBS AND BARS IN WASHINGTON DC

Elixir Nightclub: Elixir Nightclub, located in the center of downtown D.C., is a top nightlife destination recognized for its elegant environment and cutting-edge music. The club has cutting-edge sound and lighting equipment, providing partygoers with an immersive experience. Elixir features worldwide DJs with a mix of electronic, hip-hop, and top 40 tunes. Elixir is a favorite option for those looking for an expensive and exciting nightlife experience, thanks to its trendy design, VIP bottle service, and big dance floor.

Eighteenth Street Lounge (ESL): stands out as a hidden treasure in Washington, D.C. for a more casual and private ambiance. ESL is housed in a renovated home and has many rooms, each with its distinct ambiance. ESL offers it all, whether you like live jazz, reggae, or electronic rhythms. The club draws a wide variety of music fans and is noted for its excellent mixologists who create unique drinks. Eighteenth Street Lounge is a must-visit for anyone looking for a sophisticated and diverse experience, with its laid-back environment and top-notch music choices.

U Street Music Hall: Long popular among residents, U Street Music Hall remains a fixture in the city's nightlife scene in 2023. This underground club focuses on exposing developing talent in electronic music genres such as house, techno, and disco. The outstanding sound system at U Street Music Hall provides an immersive audio experience. The venue's big dance floor, informal atmosphere, and moderately priced beverages make it a popular choice for music fans and those looking for an unassuming but spectacular night out.

The Whiskey Room: The Whiskey Room at Jack Rose Dining Saloon is a must-visit for whiskey fans and those looking for a sophisticated drinking experience. The Whiskey Room, located in the Adams Morgan area, has over 2,700 whiskeys from across the globe, making it one of the greatest collections in the nation. The skilled staff is delighted to help customers through the extensive whiskey selection, guaranteeing that each guest has a unique experience. The Whiskey Room is a distinctive location for whiskey lovers and those searching for a refined bar experience, thanks to its snug and private environment and superb whiskey options.

Bruce Terry

The Velvet Lounge: The Velvet Lounge, located in the busy U Street Corridor, provides a diverse mix of live music, DJ performances, and themed events. This compact theater draws a varied clientele and takes pleasure in promoting developing and local talent. The Velvet Lounge has an ever-changing array of performers ranging from indie rock to hip-hop and everything in between. The relaxed ambiance, moderately priced beverages, and compact setting make this a welcoming location for music fans looking for a genuine and unforgettable experience.

NIGHTLIFE IN WASHINGTON DC

• LIVE MUSIC

The Anthem: Located at The Wharf, The Anthem is one of Washington DC's top live music venues. This cutting-edge facility provides an intimate but spacious environment for up to 6,000 people. The Anthem draws both renowned and new musicians from all over the globe, with performances spanning from rock and pop to electronic and hip-hop. The Anthem delivers a unique live music experience with its superb sound quality and lively atmosphere.

U Street Music Hall: U Street Music Hall is the place to go if you want an intimate and underground music atmosphere. This club features a wide variety of musical styles, including electronic, house, techno, and alternative. U Street Music Hall, known for its amazing sound system and no-frills environment, draws both local

Bruce Terry

talent and famous DJs, providing an explosive night of music and dancing.

The Kennedy Center: A trip to Washington, DC would be incomplete without seeing the cultural center that is the Kennedy Center. Aside from world-class theatrical and dance acts, the Kennedy Center also hosts an impressive array of live music events. This renowned theatre showcases a diverse range of musical acts, from classical orchestras to jazz bands and Broadway musicals.

Jazz in the Garden: Jazz in the Garden is a must-see event for music fans throughout the summer months. This free outdoor performance series in the National Gallery of Art Sculpture Garden features an eclectic mix of jazz, blues, and Latin music. Bring a blanket, a picnic, and relax in the gorgeous garden setting while listening to the wonderful songs.

The 9:30 Club is a storied institution in the DC music scene, with a long history of showcasing breakthrough concerts. This venue has hosted performances by Nirvana, U2, and Radiohead. With a capacity of 1,200 people, the club provides an intimate atmosphere for up-close and personal encounters with your favorite acts.

Bruce Terry

• ROMANTIC EVENING

Evening Stroll around the National Mall: Start your romantic evening with a stroll along the National Mall, a stunning two-mile ribbon of greenery surrounded by renowned structures. The Mall provides stunning views of the Washington Monument, the U.S. Capitol, and the Lincoln Memorial. As evening comes in, the monuments are wonderfully lighted, creating a romantic mood. Take a minute to rest on a seat or have a picnic on the Mall, relishing the tranquil environment and the companionship of your loved one.

Romantic Dinner at the Georgetown Waterfront: After your walk, proceed to the lovely Georgetown area, noted for its historic beauty and spectacular waterfront vistas. Treat your lover to a romantic supper at one of the waterfront restaurants, affording breathtaking views of the Potomac River. Indulge in wonderful meals and superb wines while enjoying the romantic setting and peaceful sounds of the sea lapping against the coast.

Potomac River Cruise: For a genuinely stunning experience, try taking a Potomac River cruise. Several firms provide evening cruises where you may enjoy a great meal, live music, and stunning views of the city's monuments from the sea. As you float down the river, you and your spouse may snuggle up and soak in the romantic ambiance beneath the starlit sky.

Bruce Terry

Romantic Walk across the Tidal Basin: One of the most recognizable sites in Washington, D.C., the Tidal Basin is particularly stunning in the evening. This lovely reservoir is flanked by cherry blossom trees, which bloom in the spring, yet the Tidal Basin's beauty transcends seasons. Take a romantic stroll along the shoreline, hand in hand, savoring the quiet ambiance and the reflection of the lit monuments on the lake.

Evening at the Kennedy Center: For couples who adore the arts, a visit to the John F. A must-see is the Kennedy Center for the Performing Arts. Catch a romantic performance such as a ballet, opera, or classical music concert in one of the center's gorgeous venues. The Kennedy Center provides a varied choice of concerts throughout the year, ensuring there is something to suit every taste.

Rooftop Bar Experience: Washington, D.C. features multiple rooftop bars that give amazing panoramic views of the city's cityscape. Visit one of these rooftop eateries and grab a romantic drink while gazing at the city lights and enjoying each other's company. The dynamic environment, mixed with stunning vistas, will produce an unforgettable evening.

Nocturnal Monuments Tour: Embark on a nocturnal monuments tour for an awe-inspiring and romantic experience. Several tour companies provide guided tours that display the lit sites, such as the Lincoln Memorial, the Jefferson Memorial, and the Martin Luther

Bruce Terry

King Jr. Memorial. Learn about the history and importance of these renowned places while enjoying the magnificent mood generated by the lights.

HEALTH AND SAFETY

Vaccines and Health Precautions: Before coming to Washington, D.C., it is good to verify whether there are any necessary vaccines or health precautions particular to your home country. Ensure you are up to date with standard vaccines and explore extra immunizations such as Hepatitis A and B, influenza, and COVID-19 shots. Consulting a healthcare expert or visiting a travel clinic can help you make educated choices regarding your health requirements.

Health Insurance and Medical Facilities: It is crucial to have proper health insurance coverage when going to Washington, D.C. Review your insurance to verify it covers comprehensive medical coverage, including emergency care. Familiarize yourself with the local hospitals, urgent care centers, and medical institutions in the region, along with their contact information, should the need arise.

COVID-19 Considerations: Given the continuing COVID-19 epidemic, it is vital to be updated about the newest recommendations and limits in Washington, D.C. check the official

Bruce Terry

websites of the Centers for Disease Control and Prevention (CDC) and the District of Columbia Department of Health for updates on travel warnings, mask regulations, and vaccine requirements. Adhere to social distancing measures and observe any special requirements imposed by local authorities.

Safe Transportation: Washington, D.C. provides several transportation alternatives, including the metro, buses, taxis, ride-sharing services, and walking. When taking public transit, keep situational awareness, particularly during busy hours. Be mindful of your things and avoid flaunting important goods. Familiarize yourself with the Metro system map and plan your journeys to avoid possible dangers.

Personal Safety: While Washington, D.C. is typically a safe city for visitors, it is vital to practice common sense and take care to safeguard personal safety. Avoid going alone in unknown regions at night and remain in well-lit, popular areas. Keep your valuables safe and be careful of pickpockets in popular tourist places. If you experience any emergency, phone 911 for urgent help.

Weather Considerations: Washington, D.C. has a variety of weather conditions throughout the year. Summers may be hot and humid, while winters can be frigid with occasional snowfall. Stay knowledgeable about weather predictions before your trip and bring suitable clothes and accessories. In severe weather events, observe local recommendations and take essential actions to be safe.

Food and Water Safety: Washington, D.C. has a diversified culinary scene, but it is crucial to consider food and water safety. Opt for reputed restaurants and cafes that keep good cleanliness standards. Drink bottled water or use a water filter if you like tap water. Wash your hands often, particularly before meals, and carry hand sanitizers for further protection.

Emergency Contacts: Save vital contact numbers, including your embassy or consulate, local police, your hotel's front desk, and medical emergency services, on your phone or a printed list. Having these contacts readily accessible can help you seek aid swiftly in case of any crises.

PHARMACY AND FIRST AID

Pharmacies in Washington, DC: Pharmacies in Washington, DC are conveniently placed around the city and provide a large variety of pharmaceuticals, over-the-counter treatments, and healthcare items. Here are a few well-known drugstore chains and independent pharmacies you may trust:

CVS drugstore: With multiple locations around the city, CVS Pharmacy is one of Washington, DC's biggest and most accessible

Bruce Terry

drugstore companies. They sell prescription pharmaceuticals, over-the-counter medications, personal care supplies, and other things.

Walgreens: Another well-known drugstore brand, Walgreens, has multiple stores across the city. Prescription drugs, health supplies, and picture services are available.

Rite Aid Pharmacy: Rite Aid Pharmacy is another reputable alternative with several locations in Washington, DC. They sell prescription pharmaceuticals, over-the-counter medications, and basic health supplies.

Independent Pharmacies: Various independent pharmacies in Washington, DC provide individualized service and a broad choice of healthcare supplies. Glover Park Pharmacy, Capitol Hill Pharmacy, and Tenleytown Pharmacy are a few examples.

Essentials for a First Aid Kit:

A well-stocked first-aid kit might come in handy during unforeseen medical crises when traveling. The following components must be present:

Basic Materials:

Bandages with adhesive (different sizes)

Adhesive tape and sterile gauze pads

Wipes or antiseptic solution

Bruce Terry

Gloves that may be discarded

Scissors and tweezers

Pins with safety eyes

Medications:

Pain remedies (such as acetaminophen and ibuprofen)

Antihistamines are used to treat allergic responses.

Antacids for heartburn or indigestion

Medication for motion sickness

Medication to treat diarrhea

Itching cream or ointment

Personal Prescriptions:

If you use prescription prescriptions regularly, be sure you have enough for the length of your vacation. Carry them in their original packaging, together with copies of the prescription and any other medical paperwork that may be required.

Other Materials:

Thermometer digital

Sunscreen with a high SPF that repels insects

Bruce Terry

Sunburn relief with aloe vera gel

Contact information in case of an emergency

Manual or guide for first aid

Additional Suggestions:

Consult your healthcare professional before your travel to address any particular health issues or to acquire further information about essential drugs or immunizations.

Research the closest pharmacies to your lodging or prominent tourist sites you want to visit so you know where to go for help if you need it.

Check the pharmacy's hours of operation, since they may change. Some pharmacies may provide 24-hour services, which may be very valuable in an emergency.

Keep your first aid kit in a convenient location, such as your carry-on luggage or backpack, particularly for excursions or day trips.

CHAPTER 7

FOOD AND DRINK

• LOCAL DRINKS

Half-Smoke Milkshake: We start our adventure with a new take on a traditional delight. The Half-Smoke Milkshake mixes the tastes of a typical half-smoke sausage, a local favorite, with a rich and creamy milkshake. This unusual drink served in a few renowned cafes and shake shops across the city, is a must-try for anyone with a sweet taste and a spirit of culinary adventure.

Rickey: The Rickey is a refreshing drink that originated in Washington, D.C. This refreshing cocktail mixes gin or bourbon, lime juice, and carbonated water. The drink is well-known for its acidic and tangy taste, making it ideal for a hot summer day. The Rickey has become an important element of the city's cocktail culture, and it can be found at a variety of clubs and lounges around the city.

DC Brau Beer: No Washington, D.C. travel guide would be complete without covering the local beer scene. DC Brau, the city's first brewery since the 1950s, provides a variety of handmade beers that encapsulate the essence of the nation's capital. DC Brau provides something for every beer aficionado to enjoy while visiting the city, from zesty IPAs to mellow stouts.

Bruce Terry

Cherry Blossom Cocktail: As the city's most recognizable natural sight, the cherry blossoms deserve their cocktail. The Cherry Blossom Cocktail is named for the lovely pink blooms that grace the Tidal Basin in the spring. This floral-infused libation often includes sake, cherry liqueur, and other pleasant components, resulting in a flavor that reflects the essence of flowering cherry trees.

Gin Rickey Ice Pop: The Gin Rickey Ice Pop is a fun and unusual spin on the traditional Rickey drink. Local artisanal Popsicle producers took inspiration from the city's favorite beverage and turned it into a frozen delight. During the summer, these alcoholic popsicles are a refreshing way to cool down while seeing Washington, D.C.'s iconic sights.

Rum Punch: Taste D.C.'s famed Rum Punch and transport yourself to the beautiful Caribbean. This delicious cocktail blends rum, tropical fruit juices, and spices to produce a flavor reminiscent of the islands' warmth and sunlight. The Rum Punch is a local favorite and can be found at various Caribbean-themed pubs and eateries.

Coffee Milkshake: The Coffee Milkshake is a delicious spin on the conventional milkshake for coffee enthusiasts in Washington, D.C. This beverage, which combines locally roasted coffee with velvety ice cream, is the ideal pick-me-up after a day of seeing the city. This thick and tasty combination is available at several coffee shops and specialty dessert places.

Bruce Terry

Chocolate City Beer: Chocolate City Beer is another important participant in Washington, D.C.'s craft beer sector. This brewery, named after the city's historical namesake, focuses on making distinctive and tasty beers that represent the city's rich culture. Chocolate City Beer provides a variety of alternatives for beer connoisseurs, ranging from hoppy beers to creamy porters.

Gin Garden: The Gin Garden is a must-try for those who enjoy a well-crafted drink. This cocktail is inspired by the surrounding area and blends gin, cucumber, mint, and other botanical tastes to produce a pleasant and herbaceous mixture. Many Washington, D.C. pubs and lounges take pleasure in their Gin Garden concoctions, which showcase the city's passion for mixology and ingenuity.

Apple Brandy: To close off our list, we move into the world of distilled spirits with Apple Brandy from Washington, D.C. This tasty brandy, made from locally produced apples, provides a sense of the region's agricultural history. Apple Brandy is a unique and genuine drinking experience for visitors visiting the nation's capital, whether savored neat or in a creative cocktail.

Bruce Terry

• STREET FOODS

Half-Smoke from Ben's Chili Bowl: A vacation to Washington, D.C. wouldn't be complete without eating the legendary half-smoke from Ben's Chili Bowl. This neighborhood staple has been offering its delectable half-smoke sausages since 1958. The half-smoke is a unique combination of pork and beef smoked to perfection and topped with mustard, onions, and Ben's famous spicy chili sauce. Enjoy this delectable delicacy at their original store on U Street or the outpost in the Ronald Reagan Washington National Airport.

Maine Lobster Roll from Red Hook Lobster Pound: For seafood enthusiasts, the Maine Lobster Roll from Red Hook Lobster Pound food truck is a must-try. Made with pieces of fresh, luscious Maine lobster flesh, this traditional New England treat is served on a buttery toasted bun. The lobster is delicately seasoned with mayonnaise and dusted with lemon juice and seasonings. You may find the Red Hook Lobster Pound food truck at numerous sites across the city, bringing the flavor of the ocean to the streets of Washington, D.C.

Ethiopian Injera and Doro Wat from DC Ethiopian Food Truck: Washington, D.C. is home to a strong Ethiopian population, and eating Ethiopian cuisine is a must for culinary connoisseurs. Head to the DC Ethiopian Food Truck, where you can eat classic Ethiopian meals including injera and doro wat. Injera is a spongy, fermented flatbread produced from teff flour, which serves as the foundation for numerous savory stews. Doro wat, a spicy chicken stew, is a popular option. The mix of injera and doro wat produces a unique and wonderful gastronomic experience.

Peruvian Ceviche from Peruvian Brothers: Peruvian cuisine has gained appeal worldwide, and the Peruvian Brothers food truck delivers the genuine tastes of Peru to the streets of Washington, D.C. Don't miss their delectable Peruvian ceviche. Made using fresh seafood, such as fish or shrimp, marinated in citrus liquids, and blended with onions, cilantro, and a hint of spice, this ceviche is a refreshing and savory delight. Pair it with their distinctive Peruvian corn and sweet potato for a comprehensive Peruvian street food experience.

Korean BBQ Tacos from Takorean: Blending the tastes of Korean cuisine with the convenience of a portable taco, Takorean is a must-visit food truck in Washington, D.C. Their Korean BBQ tacos blend soft marinated meats, such as beef bulgogi or spicy chicken, with a range of bright toppings, such as pickled veggies, cilantro, and kimchi. The mix of Korean and Mexican ingredients in a taco provides a delicious burst of flavor. Look out for Takorean's bright yellow truck and be ready for a unique gastronomic journey.

Bruce Terry

WASHINGTON DC TRAVEL GUIDE 2023-2024

CHAPTER 8

TRAVEL ITINERARY

- ## WASHINGTON DC TRAVEL ITINERARY FOR 3 DAYS

Day 1: Morning:

Start your day by visiting the National Mall, a wide green park running from the U.S. Capitol to the Lincoln Memorial. Begin at the Capitol Building and enjoy a guided tour to learn about the country's legislative process.

Walk around the National Mall, passing by notable sights including the Washington Monument and the World War II Memorial. Take your time to examine each location and learn about its historical importance.

Visit the Smithsonian Institution, the world's biggest museum and research facility. The Smithsonian provides free entry to its different museums, including the National Air and Space Museum, the National Museum of American History, and the National Museum of Natural History. Choose a few of the museums that interest you the most and spend the day visiting their exhibitions.

Bruce Terry

Evening:

After a hectic day of touring, travel to the bustling area of Georgetown. This historic region is noted for its picturesque lanes, boutique stores, and good eating choices. Enjoy a leisurely walk along the C&O Canal and explore the interesting shops and galleries in the region.

For supper, visit one of the many wonderful restaurants in Georgetown. Whether you're hungry for Italian, seafood, or foreign cuisine, you'll find a vast array of alternatives to pick from.

Day 2: Morning:

Start your day by visiting the United States Holocaust Memorial Museum. This museum delivers a compelling and thought-provoking experience, teaching visitors about the Holocaust and its influence on the globe. Bookings are encouraged since they might become packed.

Next, travel to the neighboring National Museum of African American History and Culture. This museum emphasizes the history and accomplishments of African Americans in American culture. It's an interesting and vital organization that gives a broad view of the African American experience.

Bruce Terry

Afternoon:

Visit the White House Visitor Center, situated near the White House. While public tours of the White House itself need previous appointments, the visitor center gives an insight into the history and importance of the presidential house.

Take a short stroll to the National Gallery of Art, one of the country's best art institutions. Explore its extensive collection of paintings, sculptures, and other works of art from many eras and genres.

Evening:

Explore the colorful area of Adams Morgan, noted for its unique mix of restaurants, pubs, and live music venues. Enjoy a wonderful supper at one of the foreign cafes, followed by live music or a comedy performance at one of the local venues.

Day 3: Morning:

Begin your day with a visit to the renowned Lincoln Memorial. Admire the beautiful statue of Abraham Lincoln and take in the panoramic vistas of the National Mall and the Reflecting Pool.

From the Lincoln Memorial, take a trip to the neighboring Vietnam Veterans Memorial and the Korean War Veterans Memorial. Various monuments pay respect to the troops who fought and sacrificed in various battles.

Bruce Terry

Afternoon:

Explore the lovely area of Dupont Circle. Known for its historic buildings, chic stores, and diversified food scene, Dupont Circle provides a distinct and dynamic environment. Visit the Phillips Collection, a famous art museum showcasing pieces by Renoir, Degas, and other artists.

Take a stroll or bike ride around the gorgeous Tidal Basin. This gorgeous waterfront region is especially famed for its cherry blossoms in the spring. Enjoy the tranquil settings and take in the views of the Jefferson Memorial and the Martin Luther King, Jr. Memorial.

Evening:

End your journey with a great dining experience at one of the city's premier restaurants. Washington, D.C., features a flourishing culinary culture, with choices ranging from premium fine dining places to contemporary food halls and street food sellers.

If time permits, try watching a performance at the John F. Kennedy Center for the Performing Arts. This historic cultural institution provides a broad variety of activities, including theater, ballet, and symphony concerts.

Bruce Terry

WASHINGTON DC TRAVEL ITINERARY FOR 7 DAYS

• Day 1: Arrival and Orientation

Arrive in Washington, D.C., and check into your lodging.

Start your journey with an orientation stroll around the National Mall, the city's most prominent spot. Begin at the Capitol Building, tour the National Mall, and then see the Lincoln Memorial and the Washington Monument.

Enjoy supper at a small eatery in the Dupont Circle area.

Day 2: Museums and Monuments

Spend the day touring the Smithsonian Institution, the world's biggest museum complex. Start at the Smithsonian Castle, where you may obtain information about the many museums.

Visit the National Air & Space Museum, home to intriguing displays on aviation and space exploration.

Explore the National Museum of Natural History, recognized for its enormous collection of artifacts and displays of natural history.

In the evening, visit the Tidal Basin to observe the famed cherry blossom trees (if visiting during the spring season) and take a stroll along the waterfront.

Bruce Terry

Day 3: Capitol Hill and Historic Sites

Begin the day with a guided tour of the U.S. Capitol Building, where you can learn about the history and workings of the U.S. Congress.

Explore the Library of Congress, the biggest library in the world, and enjoy its gorgeous architecture and collection of volumes.

Visit the Supreme Judicial, where you may witness judicial proceedings if in session.

Take a tour around the historic Eastern Market, a busy area with local sellers offering fresh food, arts, and crafts.

In the evening, see a play at the famous Ford Theatre or visit the International Spy Museum for an engaging and informative experience.

Day 4: Neighborhoods and Cultural Experiences

Spend the morning visiting Georgetown, a lovely district famed for its historic residences, upmarket shops, and Waterfront Park.

Visit the United States Holocaust Memorial Museum, a strong institution committed to recognizing the victims of the Holocaust.

Explore the National Museum of African American History and Culture, which celebrates the history, culture, and accomplishments of African Americans.

Bruce Terry

In the evening, come to the busy U Street area for live music, jazz clubs, and superb food.

Day 5: Arlington and National Cathedral

Take a journey to Arlington National Cemetery, where you can watch the Changing of the Guard at the Tomb of the Unknown Soldier and visit the gravesites of important personalities like John F. Kennedy.

Explore the gorgeous grounds and architecture of the Washington National Cathedral, one of the biggest churches in the world.

Visit the Smithsonian's National Zoo, home to a broad range of animals and a nice site for a leisurely walk.

Enjoy supper in the Adams Morgan area, renowned for its various eating choices.

Day 6: Day Trip to Mount Vernon

Take a day trip to Mount Vernon, the historic estate of George Washington, situated just outside of Washington, D.C. Explore the residence, gardens, and museum devoted to the first U.S. president.

Learn about the life and times of George Washington via interactive displays and guided tours.

Enjoy the stunning vistas of the Potomac River and wander around the estate's lovely gardens.

Bruce Terry

Return to Washington, D.C. in the evening and enjoy a quiet meal in the Foggy Bottom district.

Day 7: Exploring Neighborhoods and Farewell

Spend your final day in Washington, D.C. touring the areas you haven't seen yet. Consider visiting the fashionable Shaw district, the historic Capitol Hill neighborhood, or the bustling Adams Morgan area.

Visit the National Gallery of Art, home to an extraordinary collection of paintings, sculptures, and other creative works.

Take a leisurely boat excursion down the Potomac River, experiencing panoramic views of the city's attractions.

In the evening, say goodbye to Washington, D.C. with a supper at a rooftop restaurant, viewing the metropolis.

Bruce Terry

CONCLUSION

In conclusion, the Washington, D.C. Travel Guide for 2023-2024 presents a detailed overview of the lively capital of the United States. As one of the most historically important and culturally rich cities in the world, Washington, D.C. presents a wonderful combination of famous sites, renowned museums, varied neighborhoods, and a bustling culinary scene.

Visitors visiting Washington, D.C. may immerse themselves in the nation's history by touring the National Mall, home of prominent monuments and memorials such as the Lincoln Memorial and the Washington Monument. The city's profusion of world-class museums, including the Smithsonian Institution's museums and the National Gallery of Art, provides a treasure trove of art, science, and history for all ages.

The book highlights the necessity of going beyond conventional tourist destinations. Visitors may explore the distinct flavor of each area, from the fashionable and busy streets of Dupont Circle to the lovely historic enclave of Georgetown. The city's rich culinary culture appeals to all tastes, with a broad selection of foreign cuisines and regionally influenced delicacies.

In addition to its cultural attractions, Washington, D.C. features a robust entertainment scene. The book emphasizes the city's diverse music venues, theaters, and festivals, giving abundant possibilities

Bruce Terry

for tourists to experience live performances and immerse themselves in the local arts and culture.

Furthermore, the book takes into consideration the practical elements of travel, including essential information on transit alternatives, housing suggestions, and advice for traversing the city smoothly.

Overall, the Washington, D.C. Travel Guide for 2023-2024 provides a thorough resource for tourists wishing to make the most of their stay in the nation's capital. With its rich history, lively culture, and numerous attractions, Washington, D.C. provides a memorable experience that mixes education, entertainment, and adventure. Whether it's a first-time tourist or a returning traveler, this book gives them the information and insights required to make memorable experiences in this magnificent city.

Printed in Great Britain
by Amazon